Return
of the
Prodigal
Genius

Return
of the
Prodigal
Genius

by Angelyn Ray

Return of the Prodigal Genius
and Nicky and the Flying Horse

copyright © 2008 by Angelyn Ray

ISBN: 1438245149
EAN-13:   9781438245140

The author appreciates the technical assistance
provided by Moira Mann and David Thomson III

Dedicated
to all who aspire to
Wings

The author gratefully acknowledges
John Jacob O'Neill
for inspiring the title of this book
and suggesting the possibility of a return.

Nicky and the Flying Horse

... a whimsical tale of a boy -
or it could just as easily be a girl -
who invents a way of seeing the Universe.
Of course his Invention becomes part of the Inventory
now available to other travelers ...

In the Valley of the Sunrise where there are no fences and no corrals, only shelter from the hot summer sun and from the cold winter rains, there dwells in calm contentment a mare, never knowing quite why she had come there, only that she arrived one moonlit night from a distant star.

For there are memories that play in her heart, memories which shine through her eyes, of travel, of flight, of swinging and gliding and soaring about the edges of rainbowed galaxies and among star clusters, down along ribbons of constellations and up over rivers of sparkling suns.

Yet despite all these enticing memories, the horse from the heavens is content to rest in the Valley of the Sunrise that lies between the Mountains of the Moon. There is abundant food, which grows all the more for the gentle pruning when the mare takes her meals. And the cool sparkling waterfalls that flow down from the Mountains of the Moon provide more refreshment than she could ever want.

When she arrived in the valley she knew she had wings, but so content is she that should anyone glimpse her they might not notice, for she stays there serenely without a thought of flight, her wings folded along her back and sides. Only once in a while she lifts them in order to traverse the pool or a waterfall. Then she finds herself in a green flowering meadow where she hasn't gone in a while.

Other times she spreads her wings at the edge of the pool to look down at her reflection in the still, clear water. She watches while she flexes and flutters her wings, in order to remember. Then she settles down again and naps.

Sometimes she dreams, and in her dreams she recalls her journey through the heavens, and when she wakes, not knowing if the dream were of the past or of the future, or perhaps a true voyage and not a dream at all, she is still content.

So lives the horse in the Valley of the Sunrise, between the Mountains of the Moon, never lacking for companionship.

For there are butterflies and birds galore, of many colors. Especially there are the great gossamer butterflies who fan her in the summer and blanket her in the winter, and who entertain her with their splendid aerial shows that remind her of the swirling galaxies, and sometimes of the meteor showers and newly-borning stars she has witnessed from above.

And there is the little red-and-black-suited bird who hops about looking at her from atop a stone that is shaped like an angel, or from a branch of her favorite flowering, sheltering tree beside the pool, and the bird has thus become a fond companion of the mare.

There is an eagle who soars from beyond the Mountains of the Moon and lights betimes on a topmost branch of a tree that grows high on a peak, and the mare feels that she is lovingly guarded and watched over, and the whole valley, when this happens.

No human person has ever yet chanced upon the valley, no one at all. For in that far-off place there are no traveling merchants and there are no hunters, trappers, or miners.

There come sometimes rainbows reaching over the valley, and in a village down by the seacoast, one and all gather on the green behind the village to gaze in awestruck wonder at the brilliant arc of colors in the sky, a rainbow bridge that joins together the Mountains of the Moon, north with south.

And on particularly clear and starlit nights, or perhaps when the full moon hangs so close to the earth that if there were a concert played on that nocturnal orb the villagers would be sure to hear it, they gather with their pillows and their comforters on the green beneath the valley so that they will not miss the show. After the sun descends behind the western sea and the moon rises in the evening, the mountainsides collect a sheen that changes from a silvery glow to a twinkling blanket and at last, toward morning, to a veil of fine fairy dust.

Homes and gathering places in the village are not built of trees from the valley or from the mountains, for they are made of bricks that are taken, baked and raised from the very same ground where they stay, so that the earthen homes are half underground, cool in summer, warm in winter.

And the people who live there are content to stay put, venturing only a little beyond the borders of the village, as they do upon the green between the village and the valley, or along the beach that edges the sea, in order to explore its wonders and partake of whatever bounty might cast itself upon the shore.

 ow there lives in that village between the mountains and the valley and the sea a boy named Nicky, who dreamed one night of a horse winging her way among the stars, trailing across the dark sky and then through the clouds of Earth, coming at length to circle over the Mountains of the Moon that rise majestically behind the village. Nicky woke just as in his dream the winged horse glided down into the valley and disappeared among the shadows cast by the mountains in the moonlight.

It was not until the summertime when school was out and the snow had melted from the peaks, and the dream had come again and yet again, that Nicky packed himself a lunch and bade his mother goodbye. He put on his shoes - he usually went barefoot as did most villagers - and headed for the Valley of the Sunrise.

Nicky knew no one had ever visited the valley, so content were all to see the brilliance of the shining sun in the east as it rose over the valley and faithfully climbed the sky between the mountains, and they were satisfied with the rainbows, and with the travels of the silver moon and the pictures it cast upon the land as it traced the path of the golden sun. And so when Nicky set out on that summer morning to visit the Valley of the Sunrise, he from the village was the very, very first.

On the day that Nicky first visited the valley, the mare had nibbled plenty of sweet grasses, had spread and flexed her wings over the pool in order to view their reflection for only a moment before she lay down at the water's edge to doze. She lay just underneath the boughs of her favorite tree which dripped nectar at certain times of the year. At those times, the horse ate the delectable translucent blooms just as they were beginning to spill their sweet juices. Now, the tree bore only softly shading, velvet leaves for her comfort.

So when Nicky came upon the pool from a rise of rock, he saw only the still water reflecting the whimsical white clouds and the blue, blue sky, with the sheltering tree beside it, and he thought this must be the very place for his picnic.

Nicky had forgotten his dreams of the winged horse, so enchanted was he with the climb up the valley, with the way the crystal waters gurgled over the moss-covered rocks and with the enormous filmy cream-colored butterflies, big as umbrellas, with iridescent decorations, who fluttered about, fanning him. For the day had grown warm, or perhaps it was the climb up the valley.

And there was the little red-and-black suited bird who hopped on ahead and watched him from one shiny black eye or the other. All of these charming creatures, Nicky thought, were welcoming and escorting him on his way. By now he was completely enchanted with the bird and with the huge butterflies as they all came down to the tree by the pool, and there . . . ah, there . . .

He saw the horse of his dreams lying asleep with her magnificent wings folded, the tips of the feathers spread gently over the grasses at pool's edge.

➔★➔

L est he waken the magical creature Nicky sat down to stare, barely breathing, the lunch in his knapsack forgotten. The great butterflies lifted away and the bird stood off, watching, for never before had they seen a human person in the valley.

It seemed that only a moment passed, yet a sublime forever, when the horse opened her eyes and looked into Nicky's. And in the horse's blue eyes Nicky saw all the swirling travels among the jeweled stars of his dreams.

A sudden breeze riffled the tips of her feathers as she began to fold her wings, rising to stand on her feet. For she, too, had never seen a human person before, though now she was remembering some of her own dreams.

Seeing the fluttering of the feathers in the breeze, Nicky's breath caught, for never had he seen such beauty up so close.

He could not take his eyes off her. His knapsack fell to the ground as he stood and he grabbed a branch of the tree to steady himself. He had never even seen an ordinary horse before, only in picture books. But he knew as surely as he knew his own name that nowhere before in the valley was there a horse to be seen and nowhere else, surely, was there a real horse with wings! Only perhaps in picture books, but in none that he himself had seen, only in his dreams. Until now.

He put out his hand and she came and nuzzled his palm. He stroked her mane as it fell down along her neck and wafted in the soft breeze.

Who was she? And how had she come to the valley? How was he to learn?

He put his hand to his chest.

"I am Nicky," he said. "I am a boy."

The mare opened her mouth and to Nicky's further wonder and amazement, she spoke. And he understood her words!

"I am Hypatia," she said. "I am a sky traveler."

"I have seen you in my dreams, Hypatia!" said Nicky.

Apparently this was no news to Hypatia for she merely bent to drink from the pool. She turned and began to nibble a tuft of grass before she lowered herself to the ground and this caused Nicky to remember his picnic. Still he only stared.

"You are hungry," said Hypatia.

Nicky took out his banana and his sandwich for he realized that suddenly he was indeed very hungry.

It seemed like no time at all before it began to grow dark, so absorbing was the company Nicky had found in the valley. He knew he must get home. But he didn't want to say *Goodbye* to Hypatia.

"Nicky," she said as if reading his thoughts, "would you like a ride home?"

He could only blink at her.

"I can take you there," she offered.

"I don't know what my family will think," said Nicky.

"You needn't worry," said Hypatia. "No one will see me who hasn't already found me in a dream. And if they have, they will understand."

Soon Nicky was back home and it was time for bed. He looked out his bedroom window, up the valley, and thought he could hardly wait for the next day when he would be there by the pool again, visiting Hypatia.

He would not have to wait until the next day for just outside the window, as he looked, he saw a riffling of feathers. And there she was.

In no time he was on her back, his arms around her shoulders, his bare feet tucked beneath the wings that carried them both.

They gathered speed and Nicky saw all the things he had barely glimpsed in his dreams, but now with his daytime eyes. He could hear the melodic rumbling of a great planet they passed as it turned in space. Off an immeasurable distance but seeming very close there was a slowly spinning mass of lights, a galaxy, suspended. He felt the warmth of a sun as they sped by at safe range. He smelled the smells of the vast open sky and he could tell there was a new star forming where there was no sign, yet, except for the excitement of it. Perhaps he was reading Hypatia's thoughts, as she seemed to read his.

And always, underneath him, there was the strong and solid but soft, warm, and safe presence of Hypatia the sky traveler.

Nicky looked at his arms and saw the sleeves of his flannel pajamas which his mother had made for him just a little too big. He had grown into them and now they fit. He reached up and pinched his cheek. No, he was not asleep. This was no dream!

Nicky wasn't worried about his family. He had already learned that there was no worry where Hypatia was concerned. And he was with her. He looked up and ahead. Where were they going?

➜★➜

Someday I will take you to my home," said Hypatia. She surely read his thoughts for she addressed them before Nicky voiced them. "But not now. Not tonight." Still answering his thoughts, she went on. "When you come to my home it will be to stay. And it is not time."

A sizzling sound caught Nicky's ear and they curved around a comet, flashing orange and blue and white.

Finally Hypatia spoke again. "We will meet in the Valley of the Sunrise. And at night, when you wish, we will go exploring. But for now, go to sleep, Nicky. You need to sleep. And you won't miss a thing."

Nicky was silent. For one thing, he didn't know what to say. For another, he was entranced with all the breathtaking sights and sounds of the Universe, and the limitless distances which they covered with curious speed. And he knew that whether or not they spoke, Hypatia understood exactly what he was feeling.

Nicky did go to sleep that night, for he woke refreshed in his own bed in time for breakfast.

"Your trip to the valley yesterday did you good," said his mother as she squeezed orange juice. "Do you think you'll go again?"

"Yes," said Nicky, "I think I will go today."

"What did you find there so interesting?" she asked.

"Well, there are some quite big butterflies, a little bird with a keen eye who wears a black and red suit . . ." He stopped and looked up at his mother, who was just now buttering toast.

"Mother, did you ever dream of a horse, a flying horse, a horse with wings?" he asked.

She tilted her head at him. "Why, no, Nicky, I never did. Have you?" She set the buttered toast in front of him and sat down.

He took a spoonful of wild strawberry jam and spread it on his toast. "Yes, Mother, I have. I certainly have," he said. "Maybe, even, that's why it seems the valley does me so much good as you say."

"What kind of sandwich would you like for your picnic today?" she asked.

"Whatever there is, Mother, to fix easily," he replied. "And tell me if you ever dream of a horse with wings. Then I'll take you with me for a picnic up the valley."

She put peanut butter and honey between bread slices because she knew it was his favorite.

"Not today, Darling," she said, kissing him on the forehead and handing him his lunch. "Another day, perhaps, as long as it does you so much good."

Nicky thanked her while just outside he heard a whir of great wings. He took the last swallow of orange juice, gave his mother a hug, and bounded up the stairs to the door.

"Aren't you going to wear your shoes?" she called after him.

"Not today, Mother," he answered as he lifted the latch. "Not this time."

Introduction

B y the time *The Unknown Works of Nikola Tesla* emerged from *The Tesla Discourses* I had left at my sister's house, I was used to the twinkle and gentle nudge. "Go ahead, write it," and the pictures emerged to which I put words. Hence the prologue, a child's fairy tale.

The flying horse, I suppose, is a metaphor for the fantastic flights of fancy and concrete invention taken by the real historic inventor, Nikola Tesla.

Part of the legendary inventor's genius was his childlike ingenuousness which caused him to fail in the matter of conventional riches but helped to elevate the mystique he exuded far beyond his peers. Some of them did become rich and famous on a mere shadowy sliver of the genius he displayed.

He states in his autobiography, "Like most children, I was fond of jumping and developed an intense desire to support myself in the air. Occasionally a strong wind richly charged with oxygen blew from the mountains, rendering my body as light as cork and then I would leap and float in space for a long time. It was a delightful sensation and my disappointment was keen when later I undeceived myself."

Most scholars will remember Tesla's unusual affinity for the winged denizens who share our earthly home. The theme of flight reappears in the only poem he quotes in his autobiography, from Goethe's *Faust*:

> *The glow retreats, done is the day of toil;*
> *It yonder hastes, new fields of life exploring;*
> *Ah, that no wing can lift me from the soil*
> *upon its track to follow, follow soaring!*
> *A glorious dream! though now the glories fade.*
> *Alas! the wings that lift the mind no aid*
> *of wings to lift the body can bequeath me.*

For the several weeks my sister was working on the Tesla materials, she was visited by a little black-and-red bird. It pestered her by day and sometimes in the night as well, hopping at her patio doors, pecking and tapping, or sitting atop the Buddha statue on her deck, peering in her window as she worked on the manuscripts just inside. It disappeared only for brief recesses now and then, and permanently only when the work was finished.

She showed me the videos she took of her bold visitor, and I saw the evidence in the line of ordinary bird droppings it left as it paraded insistently just outside the double glass doors. During the time of its constant visits the neighborhood cats, accustomed to roaming across her garden on their regular rounds, remained strangely absent.

Our venture drew to a close and I finally quit

dodging my own responsibility, resuming my own work on the series of discourses I was privileged to record just at the closing of the last century, the results of which I present in these pages.

I have forcefully restrained myself from apologizing to the reader for the meager bounds of my own intellect, to which the unbounded mind of Tesla has chosen circumstantially to confine itself. My only academic qualification is an insatiable curiosity regarding the makeup, meaning and point of human consciousness, which has led me into the fields of mental health and psychotherapy.

An added personal qualification is an early-aroused intensity of interest in the inventor himself. It seems to me a quirk of Tesla's that he is pleased to work with me even though I am oblivious of the detailed worlds he created in his mind. Why me? Why, indeed, during his lifetime as Nikola Tesla, a New York pigeon? The man is, after all, the epitome of enigma.

If you are a scientist who grasps the concepts underlying the inventions that Mr. Tesla left behind in 1943, and if as such you would like to test my own grasp of any of those technical inventions, you needn't bother. I will only, politely, shrug my shoulders. It is not necessary to know how the chef prepared the meal in order to savor and digest it.

What is important is that the consummate inventor still speaks, or speaks again, and that he has turned his attention to the universality of the genius that resides within us all. The friend I affectionately call "Nicky T." is alive and well, I assure you, if invisible and as far as I know incorporeal these days. His humor remains. His interest in the civilization he left in 1943 goes on unabated, though those interests have undoubtedly expanded beyond humanly known realms.

John Jacob O'Neill, of whom Tesla said, "You understand me better than any man alive," and who published *Prodigal Genius* in 1944, the year after Tesla died, wrote, "Perhaps, if there is any communication from beyond the veil that separates this life from whatever exists hereafter, Tesla may look down upon earth's struggling mortals and find some way of dropping a hint concerning what he accomplished; but, if the situation is such that this cannot take place, then we must await until the human race produces another Tesla."*

It is not only my belief but my utter certainty that there is "communication from beyond the veil." I am also convinced that since the human race has, with whatever other forces were at play, already produced a Tesla, it need not repeat the act. His own play as Nikola Tesla did not end in 1943.

If I am delusional I am happily so and would not have it any other way. If I am not, this book represents nothing less than a return of the "prodigal genius" that Tesla was, and is, as he looks in upon ourselves, "Earth's struggling mortals." He turns his attention away from the technological wonders he developed and held wholly in his mind to the wonders he knows that we all hold in

---

* This quote is taken from "The Unpublished Chapter 34 of *Prodigal Genius*," by John Jacob O'Neill, accessed on the web.

our own minds. He teases them from us with a twinkle in his eye, and with his anomalous metaphors and examples.

Let me be clear: This does not claim to be a "channeled" work. Heaven forbid. This is rather a collaborative work. As with all true collaborations, the labor is expressive of both parties involved. My part is capturing the transcendent concepts and doing my best to consign them to language. His part is revealing the development of a particular hidden genius alluded to in his autobiography: "From childhood I was compelled to concentrate attention upon myself. This caused me much suffering but, to my present view, it was a blessing in disguise for it has taught me to appreciate the inestimable value of introspection... ."

The result is an elaboration of what he calls The Human Inventory.

How did such an improbable collaboration begin? At the cusp of 1997-98, late on New Year's Eve, a friend phoned me with a question. She knew of my deep interest in the works of Tesla as well as my fascination with the workings of the human mind, and that I consider my counseling practice in part a laboratory for that study. Her question was based on an excerpt from Tesla's autobiography regarding certain visual phenomena he experienced:

"In my boyhood I suffered from a peculiar affliction due to the appearance of images, often accompanied by strong flashes of light, which marred the sight of real objects and interfered with my thought and action. They were pictures of things and scenes which I had really seen, never of those I imagined. When a word was spoken to me the image of the object it designated would present itself vividly to my vision and sometimes I was quite unable to distinguish whether what I saw was tangible or not. This caused me great discomfort and anxiety. None of the students of psychology or physiology whom I have consulted, could ever explain satisfactorily these phenomena.... Such an advance would revolutionize all human relations. I am convinced that this wonder can and will be accomplished in time to come. I may add that I have devoted much thought to the solution of the problem."

The autobiography later states, "It is my eternal regret that I was not under the observation of experts in physiology and psychology at that time."

In short, my friend wanted a posthumous mental health assessment done on the great inventor who himself had in his lifetime, unsuccessfully, sought the same.

She sent me a copy of Tesla's autobiography which I read with fascination; it was my first inkling that such a document existed. Then, instead of writing an assessment based on what I found there, I posed the question to the aethers. The answers began to unfold, not as expected, but unfold they did.

The great inventor's "eternal regret" had evolved during the interim, it seemed, and he commenced imparting a newly developed psychological model of his own, with the potential to uplift the world of the human psyche as he had, in his lifetime, uplifted the world of matter and technology.

The historic Tesla represents the ultimate in both individualism and altruism, and the genius with which he blended the two qualities set the world on its ear, during his lifetime as Nikola Tesla and continuing after. He returns now to beckon us inward, each and every one of us, to where our own combined and balanced individualism and altruism are waiting to be lit by the genius residing, though perhaps dormant, within us all.

If you haven't yet, do read Tesla's autobiography, which is available on the world wide web. It is also published under the title *My Inventions, The Autobiography of Nikola Tesla* by Cosimo Classics, "as originally published in 1919." It will bridge the divide between the popularly known Tesla and the revelations you are about to imbibe.

Welcome to a new journey inward.

Angelyn Ray
2008

Chapter One

If full knowledge of the human inventory is acquired,
the human being has the basic tool kit
for development toward the ultimate mastery of matter
including one's own body.

D aughter, you have heard from many another E.T., why do you resist my speaking to you? It would be my pleasure, also my desire, to do so. This is an opportunity for me as well as for you, and for the friend who requested this writing.

You may dispense with the idea of conforming to notions of psychopathology and related diagnostic criteria regarding my autobiography, for the science of the mind generally extant today is in a stage that is best described as embryonic. Terms such as "obsessive-compulsive" in regard to the gambling, "enabling" or "co-dependent" in regard to Mother's paying for it, and "ego defense" in regard to Father's humor could be discussed, but such a discussion, even if it led to a demonstration of my being the exception rather than the rule, would occupy time and energy (light) best *invest*-ed in the *invest*-igation of other avenues.

Let me, if you please, lead you through my auto-biography and pick out certain leading phrases and events and we will see where they take us.

The opening sentences:

"The progressive development of man is vitally dependent on invention. It is the most important product of his creative brain. Its ultimate purpose is the complete mastery of mind over..." let us say over the body in which the brain is located. This would include all body functions, the autonomic, the endocrine, glandular systems, chemical interactions and all the fluid courses within the body which support the expression of the organism via thought and emotion.

If human development is indeed dependent on invention, if invention is the most important product of the brain, then what is invention? Is it the innovative design of gadgets? Is it the forward march of technology? Only in part, in very, very small part. Invention could be defined for our purposes as "venting within, the burgeoning of creation in its initial stages of manifestation."

Invention begins with *inventory*. This is also where the shortfall of modern psychology begins -- although to its credit, and the credit of the leaders of the movement, the shortfall in psychological inventory is due not to oversight, but due to the enormity of the volume to be inventoried. And since the loss and the wasting of so much essential information by various kinds of empirical or missionary crusading, inventory of vast amounts of material has been delayed while the lost components are, hopefully, located.

The nature and make-up of the human spirit and

soul, for example, shrouded in myth, mystery, doubt and faith, is easily objectified and mapped, if one knows the territory, or if one has complete inventory. After soul and spirit, mind and psyche would follow, demystified, standing aglow in all its glory. Soul and spirit would be shown to flow and mingle outside time-space while mind and psyche cover the connection between eternity and time-space, or temporal location. For our purposes, let's define eternity as "Being outside time-space."

Moving into objectivity from soul/spirit through mind/psyche, we come to the realm of emotion/motivation. While soul/spirit is outside time-space and mind/psyche covers the connection between soul/spirit and time-space, emotion/motivation is chemically glued to time-space, and the body, with all its measurable parts, systems and functions, is the burst of visible manifestation at the endpoint of each streaming impulse.

All of the systems in the human inventory must be understood in their entirety if one is to be in possession of a complete inventory of human being.

The streaming outward from universal mind through to manifestation in a human body is the path of *expression*, and the return or inward path is the path of *service*, each level serving the next. The view toward matter necessitates *expression* to that end, while the view toward universal mind necessitates *service - to that end.*

All thought originates in universal mind. Thought is the *oxylinear force field* that enters and alters reality.

THE HUMAN INVENTORY

Imagine an arc flowing between Universal Mind and Human Being (body).

$$) ( ) ( )$$
$$( ) ( ) ($$

Soul/Spirit   Mind/Psyche   ) ( )

Universal Mind   Emotion/Motivation

Human Being (body)

$$) ( ) ( ) ($$
$$) ( ) ( )$$

← ←Eternity← →Time-Space→

THE PATHS

Expression → → → → → → → → → → →

← ← ← ← ← ← ← ← ← ← ←   *Service*

THOUGHT

The *Oxylinear Force Field* that alters reality, a moving pinpoint that might lodge at any position on the diagram.

In this model of the human inventory, thought is a roving pinpoint that might lodge at any position on the diagram. As it moves outward it lets itself be the carrier of the area it enters, subject to the will there encountered.

Let us look again at the opening sentences in the autobiography: "Human development is dependent on invention, the most important product of the brain. The purpose is mastery over matter..."

If full knowledge of the make-up of the human being, from spirit through body, is gained, in other words, if inventory is acquired, what then? Then the human being has the basic tool kit for development toward ultimate mastery of matter.

What one does with one's tool kit -- well, there creation begins. There *invention* begins. And there is no limit to possibility here. Inventing, adventuring, is the right and noble destiny of every human being.

A life lived creatively is the best invention of all. There will be no duplication, for what we are approaching is the beauty of art at its highest expression, and the art of beauty in its finest form. I would not give you a list of possible forms the inventiveness might take, for the list would be endless. And every avenue pursued would lead the inventor back down the corridors of life, back to essential being, back to connectedness.

If one has a complete tool kit, that is, if one understands one's own entire make-up and being, one is free from all philosophy and religion, for one has transcended them both. One would naturally embrace knowledge of language and other essentials for communication, and by the age of fourteen, be fully equipped to function in the universe independently of all support and capable of limitless invention/creation.

Needless to say, yet it must be said, a person raised in an environment that would provide and support such an inventory acquired, ideally, by the age of fourteen -- or as it now stands, such an acquisition at *any* time in a much longer life span -- such a person would be free of any trace of psychopathology and therefore more interesting to a psychology of the future than of the present.

The next leading phrase in my autobiography may be quickly passed over: "...the inventor... is often misunderstood and unrewarded." This alludes merely to the lack of fit of the inventor/creator within the reigning societal structure.

"But s/he finds ample compensation in the pleasing exercises of personal powers and in the knowledge of being." The inventor -- the human being realizing potential -- knows. In the knowing is the connectedness with all levels of being, and in this there is boundless pleasure, fit, fulfillment. The inventor knows within, by inner experience, that no pleasure or fulfillment comes near comparison with that produced by following the trail of creative thought.

"I have already had more than my full measure of this exquisite enjoyment; so much, that for many years my life was little short of continuous rapture. I am credited with being one of the hardest workers and perhaps I am, if thought is the equivalent of labor....

"Every effort under compulsion demands a sacrifice of life-energy. I never paid such a price. On the contrary, I have thrived on my thoughts." This is simple, gospel, truth. It is a factual retrospective accounting of the internal experience of the inventor.

Again I say the inventor has his or her inventory in tow and is therefore cognizant of his/her own powers and potentialities. Those studying many of the esoteric sciences and histories, the ancient calendar systems, pyramids and the like, are in the process of locating longlost components of the human inventory. As the parts are located the inventory is filled out, and when it is filled out the authentic invention/creation can begin.

Yet it is not up to the individual to wait for the globally effective discoveries, but to delve *within* for the longlost components lying under the layers of silt there. Much authentic invention now offered by genius is but a meager foretaste of the flowing unfolding of genius in art and technology, the breathtaking kaleidoscope of wondrous and beauteous formations yet to be made manifest by the fulfilled human.

"I grew up with little confidence in myself," *confidence* referring to "fidelity within, and to the inner process." This statement is a typical one, presenting, with the above statements, the juxtaposition of features faced by the inventor/creator of the age, of this present order. For one's experiences in the outer world, most if not all one's contacts, when young, with authority figures and role models, negate the inner pleasure. So confidence is cut off before it can take root. Eventually, the "growing up with little confidence" gives in to no fidelity to the inner process. Or in fortuitous cases, the "little confidence" survives and later takes root and thrives, as it did in my case.

Even so, the "fit" was rough, the fit in society, for

the inventiveness carried me and supported me in endeavors that opposed the prevailing mindset and worldview of my day, even though at the same time it greatly fit and boosted to a new level the prevailing technology of my day. The fit, and lack of fit, is reflected in the acceptance, and lack of acceptance, of my name, today.

For one thing, "if work is interpreted to be a definite performance in a specified time according to a rigid rule, then I may be the worst of idlers." The Puritan work ethic is still popularly revered. I did not fit or fulfill it. And since the means to my ends -- thought leading to invention -- was invisible and unfitting to the scrutinizing judge of the day, the end itself was suspect. And even though the inventions, presented fully developed rather than through agonizing, laborious trial and error, proved their own worth, even that proven worth was somehow unacceptable -- and, yes, still is -- because it came with ease rather than through arduous task-minding. The ease, mind you, refers to the pleasure and completeness of the inner process, and is not at all associated with idleness, indeed, is the antithesis of idleness.

Now, many people seldom dislodge thought from body. Others seldom dislodge thought from emotion/ motivation. Still others have difficulty bringing thought *into* time-space, but cast it into the realms of mind/psyche or soul/spirit as often and for as long as they can. A balanced human being is in command of thought, meaning that thought *plays* freely and creatively to and fro, from universal mind through all the worlds into the body, back and forth, at will. And the will in this balanced individual, if playing through all the spheres, is in harmony with universal mind and therefore in conformity to all the laws of love.

I use the word "play" intentionally. The "rapture" and "exquisite enjoyment" I experienced, "thriving on my thought," is play of the highest order. It is *freedom* of thought that makes way for the healthful joy and rapture.

I submit that human misery of any stripe and description can be traced to the failure to free the thought. Thought, being naturally mobile, roving, free, when held on a leash, no matter how long, becomes a captor itself, captivating the thinker and holding him or her hostage. In actuality, the first hostage was the thought itself, bound, which in turn binds the thinker who bound it.

Invention/creation issues from the one who lets thought rove freely, then, not in other people's business, but in one's own business. And one's own business is one's own inventory of all one's sacred parts and inheritance, from soul/spirit on into and through the body.

Now I have said that each level moving *from spirit to body* seeks expression. So thought, emitted from universal mind, may enter the realm of soul/spirit where it is attracted by a modicum of spirit ready to express universal mind. That soul/spirit then travels via thought into the realm of mind/psyche where it is further encapsulated and gathers ideas and ideals. Since the direction of motion is that which seeks, or moves toward, expression (spirit to body), the mind/psyche then moves thought toward the realm of emotion/motivation, gathering there the impetus into matter, into body.

Once in body, thought can be held captive, but the impulse, spirit having found expression now, is movement back to universal mind through service. If the body-bound spirit forgets, the captivity begins. However, if thought is not taken captive in the body but allowed its natural mobility, the body will serve the emotion/motivation. If thought is there taken hostage, all kinds of dangerous situations may result. However, if service flows, the body with its emotion/motivation will serve the mind/psyche. If thought is allowed no further release the danger is less, but there is apt to result a wasteland for the individual. Thought allowed freedom in mind/psyche, however, will rove back to serve the soul/spirit, and soul/spirit being neighbor to universal mind, thought is then free to anchor again at home base, fulfilled, or may begin again its search for expression.

Let us look at the upbringing of a child raised to be independently inventive by the age of fourteen. This can be outlined very briefly for the process is simple. The difficulty lies in initiating and maintaining the simplicity, for current societal structure is a long way from supporting the required fundamental simplicity.

The child's family may be a nuclear family or it may be any combination of adults. The criteria to be met is a group of well-rounded individuals with at least one adult *per child*, preferably two or more adults to one child in each familial setting.

Birth to 3½ years. The child's physical needs are completely met. Food, temperature, comfort, drink, all are tended to in the most diligent and knowing way. The senses are stimulated pleasantly, artfully, and in a most nurturing fashion. Emotionally, the child is sheltered among people of varying ages, who are good humored, stable and secure in their own emotional well-being. Any crying or humor, any emotional display from the child will be received without censure. The child is kept often among adults who are in the acts of artfully creating. Mindfully and psychically, the child needs only this and the mind and psyche will develop according to the inner potential of the child.

3½ to seven years. The above is continued, and the child is now encouraged and supported in play that capitalizes on the imagination of the child and on the expression of fundamental and subtle nuances of emotion, drawing from the real life experiences of the child. Costume, fantasy, nature and explorations in nature are emphasized.

Seven to 10½ years. The above nurturing environment remains stable. Learning of technical arts and sciences, language and philosophy is introduced at seven and continued through this and the next period. In philosophy and history, theories and questions are brought out, leaving the children to their own interpretations and expansion of ideas. Children of like temperament are placed together, thereby providing the environment for them to hone any personal excesses and correct any deficiencies.

10½ to 14 years. The nurturing environment established in the first seven years has continued. Emphasis on education continues from the previous 3½ years, while following the particular individual interests of each child.

Next, we will consider the play of folly.

Chapter Two

*Folly is any slippage from the beaten, well-ordered path,
hence, wild card, serendipity, the field of exercise
for the human free will, necessary to any invention/creation,
because there is no invention in the beaten,
well-ordered path.*

I could speak more to you of myself, myself as symbol, as illustration, *not* as example or as master.

Mastery is a relative term, relative to one's point of view. Every master in one field is a beginner in another. So I am a master and a beginner as well, as are you and everyone else. The human danger lies in the tendency to apply one's sense of mastery to areas where one is in actuality a beginner. Therein, one might say, lies all folly.

It is equally fallacious to act as a beginner when one is actually in mastery, though this is less common. Yet many gifts are this way squandered, which in some ways was my folly, squandering my "inventions" as if I were a beginner practicing with toy parts. I applied a beginner's mentality, in a sense "beginner's luck," to a field of technological mastery, considering the state of technological development then extant. What were the alternatives? I don't believe there were alternatives. Folly is part of the force field of Earth -- the wild card, the free will, serendipity, the lottery.

So let's talk about folly. It rhymes with jolly, trolley, golly, holly, terms that evoke joy and whimsy. Folly has been attached to the notion of foolishness. Let's say for our present purposes that folly is any slippage from the beaten, well-ordered path, hence, wild card, serendipity, the field of exercise for the human free will. If everything proceeded along the beaten, ordered path, then where is the exercise of human initiative? I fell off the path, way off, and never got back on.

Folly also rhymes with brawly, crawly, volley, and it can be that, too, but need not be. Folly is a highwire, a tripwire, a livewire. Where would we be without it? The doldrums, I suspect. So let's hear it for folly. Folly is necessary to any invention/creation, because there is no invention in the beaten, well-ordered path. Nor could we have folly alone. Folly and order are two sides of the coin of living. Mr. and Ms. Folly and Order. They need each other; they can't live without each other.

Let's define *folly* as "human foible," and *foible* as "a guarantee of human authenticity." Everyone has access to the light and sound spectrum in its entirety. However, when one enters human life through the conventional gauntlet -- human conception and birth -- one agrees to focus within the narrow known bands.

Do you know how a virus works? It enters the system and injects change at the molecular and cellular levels. Say human beings are like viruses. They come into the known band of human knowing and each one injects change in that stratum. Some inject a greater amount of change, some a lesser, but all bring the capacity to alter the entire organism. Avatars and tyrants alike have done so.

What did I inject? I injected knowledge of technology brought in in a spiritual manner. I set the example of material/technological evolution made possible through the opening of the mental faculties to the spirit.

Take the diagram of the human basic inventory. When technological advancement occurs in a normal limited way the human works with motivation and mind on that chart. Universal mind, soul/spirit, psyche, and emotion are left out. Do you see how this works? This manner of so-called evolution has spawned the widespread use of computers which also employ mind and motivation, most often to the exclusion of universal mind, soul and spirit, psyche, and emotion.

How is psyche typically omitted from technological development? The psyche is the formative principle which develops the sparks sent out by universal mind. The psyche is omitted when mind operates independently of the spark. A spark from universal mind can be cloned by mind and may seem to bear the universal life force. But the clone cannot bear the life force, or the spirit or soul. Therefore the clone operates in the realms of mind and motivation, the motivation driven by history in the realm of technological development. See the difference? The difference between a locomotive running on power and one coasting downhill. Or the difference between a butterfly in flight and one pinned under glass.

The psyche enlivens mind. The psyche provides

the critical connecting link between the realms of eternity and the realm of space-time. Or between soul/spirit and emotion/motivation. Mind provides the substance and psyche provides to mind the yeast. Psyche contains the breath of life, the secret ingredient that enlivens and inspires the substance of mind.

All of this feeds into motivation. If motivation is bereft of soul/spirit, of psyche, and even of its own counterpart, emotion, it receives the input of a clone, which cannot grow and develop but can only put out what was once put in it, a closed book, a finished work, a stagnant pool.

Are you beginning to grasp the import of the inventory and the importance of utilizing all its parts in sync? And seeing how its relegation to disregard and contempt has led humankind to its critical pass? To say nothing of the effects on politics and economics. Do you see how emotion and psyche, denied, run rampant via misuse of human intimacy in the media? The denial breeds misuse, abuse, perversion, just as repression breeds obsession. And do you see how in economics, desire -- a natural component of motivation when joined with emotion and psyche -- runs rampant and breeds perversion, abuse and misuse, commonly known as greed, hoarding, avarice and the like, because emotions such as compassion and empathy are blocked and thus the psyche is prevented from serving the spirit on its return to universal mind?

How does my method differ? I used all the parts of the basic inventory. I used human being (my being as I was), motivation and mind. I also used emotion but not as one might think, that is, rather than putting emotion on hold while working in the lab, then going home and kicking the dog, so to speak, I burrowed through emotion as an earthworm burrows through dirt, taking it in completely, expelling it and then burrowing on in the same fashion.

In order to employ emotion one must steep in it, revel in it, BE IN IT, as I was as I appeared to be daydreaming. The act of emoting is not evidence that one is feeling. True experiencing of one's emotions occurs within a still vessel. Denial of emotion forces the body to develop symptoms. Acceptance of emotion allows the body to function normally, while within, the emotion is explored with great curiosity and interest.

I did this, feasting on the emotional banquet arrayed within, the ever-changing internal weather. When fear, anger, joy or sorrow presented themselves to me, in varying combinations or in their many variations, in awe, wonder and admiration I embraced the feeling, for I always accepted emotion as a great treasure peculiar to humanity. I would not squander it, demean it or deny it but devour it and savor it to the last aftertaste. Pain, no different. Elation, the same.

You see why praise and acclaim were irrelevant to me. They could not hold a candle to the stimulation of my own internal landscape. I was inner focused, not outer, and brought forth the inventions I patented from my inner store with little regard to what might happen once they were brought forth, beyond the satisfying acts of patenting and the personal contacts I carried on.

If humans would so value and so tend the beautiful gardens of their own emotional being, ongoing like weather, creativity and inventiveness would flourish. This is how emotion is transcended. It is accepted, loved, explored, and then, in the end, it is transformed into powers little dreamed of.

Let us dwell for a moment with situations wherein a relationship is carried on with a taboo element, where an aspect of a relationship or an emotional attraction is taboo, in some way or other socially censured. The social condemnation provides an entire category of emotions not otherwise available in the same relationship. Therefore everyone at one time or another partakes of a taboo or these emotions peculiar to bucking the tide of society cannot be experienced. For example, when I bucked great currents of water as told in my autobiography I developed strength I could not have without the forceful opposition -- strength, stamina, fortitude, in spades.

Then why doesn't my autobiography record such human relationships? Perhaps they are simply not recorded. Perhaps they occurred, or are occurring in a different time-space corridor. I will say that no emotional experience is left unknown to one committed to learning the transcendence of emotion.

I went in human experience where my emotions led me and you must do the same. Now the same emotion may lead each of us to a different pass. From each emotional moment there are many possible directions. So here we are again, right where we began, human foible, folly.

If it is your folly to be drawn by us here, to be drawn *by your own developing spirit*, then you shall be drawn. It cannot be otherwise. You are not unique or special any more than anyone else who comes this way. Yet it is just as true that you are of infinite specialness and uniqueness. For the stuff of human life is infinitely special, infinitely unique. How does it differ from the stuff of other life? Of animal life on Earth? Of life even here, where I am with these others? It differs in this way: the specialty of human life is its relationship to CHOICE. There is free will. There is folly. And in that is the mandate to be fully human.

How to be fully human? To follow the creeds, codes and mandates of certain other humans? That is how to violate, distort, contort humanness. Then, to reproduce and bear many children, new human beings? That is how to maximize the distortions, not the humanness.

For while the mandate to humanness is the mandate to folly, the other mandate of humanness is the blockage of free will. There are many such blocks, many mandates to outlaw folly. Look around you. Laws maintain order and there is merit in this, the human condition being what it is, otherwise we would have mere disorder. However, most laws are set up to mandate conformity to social norms. Very few actually protect the vulnerable and disarm the aggressor. The expression of free will is curbed by these blocks to its free expression.

Folly is not disorder. Folly is the essential counterpart of order. Folly is the friend of order, not its antithesis. How is folly the friend of order? There is order in a cemetery; there is order in a deck of cards, order in a file cabinet, order on a map. To bring folly into the picture is to bring life to the cemetery, to bring players to the deck of cards, file clerks to the file cabinet, and travelers to the map. Folly and order are the two necessary partners in human life.

Is order itself the block to folly? No, order is the partner of folly. The blocks to folly are directly focused on snuffing out the possibilities presented by the following of folly on the part of willing -- free-willing -- human beings.

For example, the child in the nursery plays randomly and whimsically. That is folly. The order is provided by the nurse, who lovingly dresses the child, takes it to meals, tucks it in for its nap. That is folly and order acting as partners. The blocks, then, to folly, would come in the form of the nurse who, having been blocked from her own play in her own childhood, would restrict the child's play in honor of restriction rather than in honor of the child's safety and nurturance.

There are many such blocks to folly: the politician who seeks to mandate others' private lives, the teacher who squelches creativity, the parent who "breaks" the child's spirit in honor of the parent's own broken spirit, the government which protects its power through levying inordinate taxes and fostering unholy wars, the priest who fosters fear and guilt in his "flock," the doctor who prescribes medication in lieu of healing, who performs surgery in order to experiment. Well, then, isn't folly furthered in the lives of the politician, the teacher, the parent, the government, the priest, and the doctor? Yes, but...

The *true* block to folly, the block that comes from beyond the human condition, that comes out of universal law is: the law of love, which calls for the telling of new stories without the negation of another's story. And here comes a qualification to that true block to folly, and here is the paradox: It -- the law of love -- is not a block at all, but represents the systematic expansion of the numbers of stories. For if one is to create a new story in the universe, say, one is to learn one's own healing, one is negating the story of the drug-or-surgery-happy doctor, isn't one? No, one is creating a new option in the universe, increasing the numbers of options, different than negating a story.

The negation of a story entails the forceful curtailing of the lifeline of a living being. The one who learns self-healing creates a new option, but if he or she were to take a gun and go shoot the doctor who practices drug therapy or surgery when healthier options are available, that would be negating the doctor's story. See the difference? We could go through many such examples and still not cover the one you will think about next in your own life.

The beauty -- and the purpose -- of folly is that it requires choice. Not clear choice. Clear choice would be if you had to cross the Columbia River at its widest point and your only options were to swim across it or take a safe and ready motorboat. That would be a clear choice requiring nothing but a quick intellectual measurement.

The kind of choice that enhances the laws of folly would entail something like this: the options would include hang-gliding from a cliff across the Columbia at its widest point, swimming, or going upstream to find a narrower passage. Now you would have to assess your swimming skill, your skill at hang-gliding, the possibility that the winds would dump you in the water, how far upstream you might have to travel to find a spot, maybe get hold of a canoe, maybe even, if you're lucky, find a bridge, or ask around about the possibility of an existing bridge located beyond sight, even, maybe, downstream. In other words, your free will now has a playing field, and you have a chance to develop.

The clear choice does not present either the playing field for free will, or the chance for development. The alternate scenario provides many rich and poignant emotional excursions *inward* -- the stuff of which human advancement is made, the stuff of free will, of folly, of following the map to completion. That is the quest, the adventure; that is the awakening, the fulfillment of humanness.

As the floods come and that which is flooded turns into a new state of being according to the laws written within it -- the natural laws, the laws of its nature -- so the folly in one's environment changes the states of being of the one in the midst of the circumstances, states of being which unfold according to one's inner design and nature. Fires do the same, winds and earth the same as they overwhelm whether slowly or suddenly. So nature changes nature, the greater law altering the lesser law and bringing into manifestation the inner condition of the outer.

The Columbia River illustration is more a metaphor than an example. For these days the challenges come while one sits before a computer monitor, in the board room, in the bedroom. They come on the commuter flight, the track field. Nevertheless they come, and they challenge the emotions, the heart, the spirit, the soul. They challenge the human BEing to BE all it can BE.

And when it has been all it can be, what happens next? Where does it go? Where have all the human beings gone who have fully exercised free will, mastered the inner landscape, and moved on?

Chapter Three

I knew that tremendous potential lay in every moment,
in every atom, in every breeze, in every thought,
and from time to time that knowledge manifested
and my physical view was filled with the literal sight
of the bare fields of possibility.

L ight in human space-time is like molten gold, running liquid through the veins of matter. It hardens, or congeals, and is no longer light, congealing in phenomena such as color, texture, perspective. So long as it remains molten it flows (at the "speed of light") but as it hardens it slows and is transformed into visual phenomena.

Sound is the same. Sound and light often give off joint messages, such as "Look out, a train is coming!" Or "The pot is boiling over!" or "I want to attend this concert."

So long as sound continues to travel unimpeded it remains sound, as in sound waves. When it stops it can be heard and its form has changed. Heard, it is identified with matter and conveys messages such as, "A car is coming,"

"The baby is crying," or "It's time to get up, the alarm is ringing," "Someone said they love me," "I need to tend to this message." So sound crashes against matter and shatters into its parts and pieces, which are picked up and treated through the human device of folly.

Light likewise. It runs about manifestations of matter, slows, and as it congeals in visually perceived phenomena it serves as the medium of invention. Freed then, off at the speed of light, it will serve another purpose, another, and another. While light is congealed in the corridor of space-time, human folly manipulates the hardened pieces and parts, such as, "This cloth would make a lovely coat," "This car needs to be washed," or "painted," or "repaired" or "junked." "I want to know him" or "her." "I will walk this way, beside the river, not that way, up the mountain."

So the part of folly. Remember that folly and order are complementary halves of the same. It is a mistake -- a take that is missed -- for one to take the position that folly and order rule out each other. Yin and Yang. Two halves of a whole order. Yes. Folly is half of the order; order is the other half.

Congealed light and sound can be treated with order: "The child needs to learn to read. Let's do our ABC's." Or with folly: "Let the child run outside and tumble in the grass" or "autumn leaves" or "snow." The child learns equally from established human principles and from its own whimsical, unstructured explorations into inner space and the surrounding world.

It was through the folly I had well learned as an eccentric inventor that I came into the graces of those disposed to further my knowledge of myself. For the light that I saw as a child, injecting images into my objective reality, was a manifestation of myself and as such it turns out that only I could interpret it.

For knowledge of any sort is an extension of self-knowledge. Knowledge of the ABC's is an extension of one's capacity to articulate the inner landscape. Knowledge of basic mathematics is an extension of one's grasp of one's connection to the cosmos. Knowledge of geography, science, liberal arts, history -- whatever field you can name -- is an extension of what one already is, furthering the fulfillment of one's potential.

The flower germinates from the seed, which cannot show the end result without the flowering process. So the flowering human being begins from the seed, and whatever stimuli draws forth the potential in the seed, it can only draw forth what is already present but not yet manifest. So the human being only brings forth what is already encoded within. That is the part of order.

Do you see where this is leading? Every phenomenon experienced in objective reality is a manifestation of what already is, in seed form, within the sentient being. It is through folly that one stumbles into the fields of infinite possibility.

When I saw unusual displays of light which obscured objective reality, I was bringing forth the lighted void and viewing it, though unknowingly. As in my paradigm of life on Earth I knew that tremendous potential lay in every moment, in every atom, in every breeze, in every thought, from time to time that knowledge manifested and my physical view was filled with the literal sight of the bare fields of possibility. Bare, not barren. Bare, and pregnant with infinite possibility. Coding is within; creative/inventive possibility is infinite, literally, beyond belief. The most fantastic works of art, the most far out science fact and fiction, could not contain the flights of imagination that might issue from the fields of lighted possibility.

The tiny points of light that you see from time to time, like tiny flashlights turned on in the dark, are products of yourself, too. As the fields of light were products of my own proximity to the field of all possibilities, your lights are products of your knowledge of closeness to divine light, divine guidance, helping you know truly what you already know subtly, mirrored back to you now through your eyes.

The light is the stuff of creation. "Let there be light. And there was light." This is the beginning of creation, of invention. So here we are back at invention. And folly. Folly is the self-permission granted to FOLLOW. Follow what? Follow your folly. So long as it does not negate another's story, so long as it does not "offend a little one," my advice is, "Follow your folly," which is really not so different from Joseph Campbell's "Follow your bliss." What then is the difference?

Following one's bliss gives permission to do what one likes rather than what one must, pursuing joy rather than duty, fulfilling creativity rather than dull drudgery. Following one's folly gives permission to experiment while one seeks one's bliss. Following one's folly means that one is not held hostage to self-blame, self-judgment. If one is okay with the idea of following her folly, she may stumble but she will get up and go forward, knowing that the fall brought her an experience that was in itself valuable. Falling will not trouble one who follows her folly, but will only enhance her experience of herself.

Why have I chosen the word "folly"? Could it not as well be "play" or "whimsy" or "frivolity" or "spontaneity"? Not really, because through usage each of those have fallen into their own kind of predictability, though each remains somewhat applicable. "Chaos" as well, though it has come to refer more to universal law, and I wish to emphasize the role of human free will as it plays out, hence: *folly* it is, for now at any rate. In time even folly will fall into its own predictable order and then we will have to find another term, won't we?

Do you recall the shape of the Mandelbrot Set? Mysterious, complicated yet simple, primeval, organic, feminine, strange. Yet out of its consistent order, chaos flows in utter beauty. Yet the chaos is order of the highest order, so to speak, so far beyond humanly perceptible order that it is labeled "chaos." In the same way, human orderliness is chaos when viewed from a higher perspective.

What is the purpose of all this? What is the destiny/destination of it all? How to bring purpose and destiny/ation into alignment? For if destiny/ation does not align with purpose then purpose is unfulfilled, and if purpose does not align with destiny/ation, then destiny is unfulfilled and one's destination is never reached.

And so one must know both. One must be intimately involved with one's purpose, and infinitely mated with one's destiny/ation. Without the intimate involvement with purpose, one is scattered, fragmented. Without the mating with destiny/ation one is ever off the mark, ever reaching goals not to one's taste.

So what do you want? The order of purpose/destiny/ation that conforms to the orderliness of common human expectations? Those satisfied with the common order generally feel satisfaction. Or do you want the order of purpose/destiny/ation that conforms to the orderliness of the higher orders labeled chaos?

If you feel chaotic, restless, uneasy, confused, you may be swimming in the chaos and trying to make it conform to your common expectations of order. Those satisfied only with the higher orders generally feel chaotic as they struggle to achieve a sense of meaning and satisfaction in an impossible milieu, in a world of trite trivia, like the fly caught between the swatter and the wall.

The point is, human free will *is* in itself a universal law and the scale of unpredictability due to human initiative opens infinite possibility in an ordered universe. And that, in an acorn, is why E.T.'s are so interested in the human population.

Is there no free will elsewhere, other than in the human realm? Why, yes, there is, but this is for a different discussion. All of us here draw all of you there, and the only criterion is that you are willing -- there is free will. Mastery of these principles lets one step foot consciously outside. The corridor walls and ceiling give way. The floor remains, for you can alight at any time you wish. Merely, you can disembark at any time you wish.

What brings the human to the time-space corridor, and what holds one to it?

Every being coming forth into sentience on Earth

comes with a contract. The basic clause of the contract in order to gain entry to human life runs along these lines: "Till death us do part, I shall bring what I already know into manifestation in this sphere of life, and I shall learn through mixing that which I already know with that which comes to me that I seem not to know." The known is order; the unknown, infinity. The interface between these two is folly, human free will.

Hitler? It could apply. Jesus? Gandhi? Mata Hari? To whom might it not apply? What did Hitler bring that he already knew? Much pain, no doubt. What did Jesus bring? Anyone else? If the coming of one into the human condition does not produce learning for that one, but at the same time it produces much learning for others, then that one has not signed the contract, and that one, though appearing human, is not of the human strain.

What if one is a tyrant and stubborn in his or her bitterness? Well, then, what can we say about that? Do we know exactly what knowledge was brought in, and exactly how that knowledge mixes with circumstance? It would be better for us not to judge, but to apply our attention to our own folly, to our own fulfilling of our own contracts.

So learning is the basis of the human contract, and from that basis many variations occur. Some commit to certain tasks, others to helping certain others, some to acquiring a single experience. Whatever the clauses of the contract agreed to by the one entering human life, they will be based on *what one already knows*.

Most people are immersed in objective reality and do not see beyond it. And most people only see what is scientifically measurable. But *most people*, if they could or would go back far enough in memory, would *remember* "subjective" phenomena that would knock their socks off, invisible playmates the least of it. Most would remember landscapes and beings that could not possibly have their sources on Earth. Babies learn language, and while learning language they forget other worlds. So that which they already know swiftly narrows to what is commonly known on Earth. Then they begin to "grow up."

Too bad? Not really. Because the field of possibility has to be stringently limited in order for the being to concentrate on the learning needed. The lab is necessary, and the confinement of the microscope, in order to understand the greater workings. The personal is the key to the universal, the microscopic to the cosmic.

What has this to do with the human inventory? Quite a bit. In order to understand one's inventory, one needs also to understand its limitations, and that, in context with the whole. What has this to do with the diagram? Motivation. The motivation that feeds the emotions and impels one into physical manifestation is driven by the contract.

So you see how the task of the human being is to honor the contract while taking in new data, new experience, to honor accumulated knowledge while weaving in new. Every scrap of material can be used, and if this is done one lives in a continuum of synchronicity.

The question arises: Why are human beings separated from conscious knowledge of their own contracts? Let me put it this way. If knowledge is power, and if one has the power of the knowledge of the contract, one has already completed the journey. Then was the journey complete when the contract was made? No, because in order to make the unknown known the journey must be taken. The earthworm, in order to aerate the earth, must burrow through it. The human, in order to glean the benefit of the unknown, and to make the unknown known, must forge through it *unknowingly*. Each moment must entail a revelation, every step a discovery.

Think of it this way. What would happen if you were to set out on a trip and bury your nose in the map? Have you ever tried to read a road map while driving? Pretty difficult; pretty dangerous. You check the map and then travel to a certain point before checking it again. Each checkpoint is an assessment of how far you have gotten, how far you have to go, and how you will proceed next.

So each lifetime is the stretch between checkpoints on the map. You "forget" the contract so you can pay attention to the road. Might you stray from your last reading of the map, from your contract? You might, but not far. And any straying will bring new knowledge. You notice we are back again at folly.

Folly is open-mindedness; it is brainstorming. Folly is rain on a 4th-of-July parade. Is the IRS folly? Of course. Is church folly? Certainly. Folly is the unexpected rainbow, the "stranger across a crowded room" that brings you your completion just when you have become content with the journey. Let's hear it again for folly.

The difference between fact and reality, between knowledge and experience, between data and wisdom is the difference between playing house and being a householder, between star gazing and star visiting, between the one-hour documentary and settling down to live in the place for seven years.

How are fact, knowledge and data the lesser? Where then is the power of knowledge? Reality, experience and wisdom provide the land, water and air for voyaging, knowledge of facts and data the map. You can see then the importance of each, the map and the voyaging, each in its own way, to reach completion.

When one begins a journey there is an expectation that it will end, for a beginning implies an ending. Now, there are little beginnings and little endings, middle-sized beginnings and middle-sized endings, and there are great beginnings and great endings. What comes before the beginnings and after the endings? Whatever is greater than what came between the beginning and the end.

Chapter Four

*It is no accident, or coincidence, that the word curiosity
and the word cure are derived from the same root.
And what a cure! All possibilities are explored;
all potentialities become known.
And then choices can be made.*

L ove plays havoc with human free-will, for love is the compatible co-existence of all stories without the nega-tion of one by another.

A human enacts a story. Another negates it. This is the exercise of free will, isn't it? Well, it is the exercise of free will, and at the same time it is the canceling of free will -- the free will of the first story-teller, so to speak. What would happen if no story was canceled? What would happen if the neighbor's dog deposits feces on your yard, and rather than asking it to be removed, yelling at the neighbor, putting up a fence or in some other way negating the neighbor's dog's story, you became creative? Do you have any idea what wealth may be extracted from doggy doo? What if you carefully collected it and experimented with it scientifically and came up with a new brand of fertilizer that became very popular? Or even if you cheerfully washed it into your yard so that it could nourish the grass? Then there would be two uninterrupted stories.

What about violence? Rape, torture? These kinds of offenses against human others negate the stories of the victims, catapulting them into the enactment of different stories, coercing them into taking on the hidden stories of the offenders. The offenders externalize their own stories which are carried at an unconscious level, committing acts which transfer those unconscious stories to their victims. The original stories of the ones offended are eclipsed by the stories of the offenders. Whole families, whole nations, a whole world may be drawn into acting out the story of one offender.

In even these kinds of cases love is extracted, because the victims, though feeling no love for the offenders, nevertheless relinquish their stories to the stories of the offenders. So love proceeds. So long as stories continue, so long as human enactments of life continue, love wends its way through eternity.

In reality there must be some who negate the stories of the offenders. A rapist or murderer must be stopped. Here again is the principle of free will. Those who stop the offenders make their own choices, whether to honor the original stories of the victims or the imposed stories of the offenders, but primarily, how to honor and enact their own stories which mingle with those of the victim and of the offender. These are individual matters and must remain so in order to honor all we have said about following one's folly, free will, and the law of love.

Let's talk about sanity.

Sanity. Sane. Same. Settled. Sanitarium. Rest. Equilibrium. Sanity is the state of sameness, of a consistent, coherent code of reality agreed upon by the masses in conformity to leadership. Sanitation. Laundered thoughts. No one wants their "dirty laundry" aired to public view. Why not? Everyone dirties their laundry. It is the human condition to do so. So here we are back at folly. Dirty laundry is human folly. Why hide it? Why not all go to the river together, laughing, and combine washday with a grand picnic rather than hide it as if only you among all the billions don't have any dirty laundry.

Skeletons in the closet. Where do they come from? A burglar burgles your house and deposits a skeleton in the closet, to be hid forevermore? No. Skeletons in the closet come from bodies, secretly killed and hidden away. Bodies of truth, precious treasures of experience, stashed away and ignored whenever possible.

The human route to self-destruction does not come out of over-population, or even out of human greed or lack of compassion. No. The human dilemma comes from denial. Denial of the real. Denial of the painful. Denial of human folly and the beauty and wealth of it. Without it who would we be? Clones. Automatons. Good little "Christian" soldiers. So let's hear it again for folly.

Denial of the human right to folly, to experimentation with emotion and pushing the limits of experience (one's own, not another's) is the very thing that negates the story of human evolution and turns it about to self-destruction. So let's get comfortable with the idea of folly, of human foibles, of serendipity, of spontaneity in its purest meaning. What is its purest meaning? Consider Mother Earth, Mother Nature.

Mother Earth spontaneously dances to the rhythm of the spheres, keeping perfect order with all her heavenly cohorts. And Mother Nature brings spontaneous perfection to the earth through her rapturous whimsy and her displays of color, of feeling, expressed as weather. If you want to know spontaneous emotional expression, tune in to your Mother Nature. This is folly at its best balanced with order: Mother Earth. If you don't get it, take some time with these wonderful mothers, observing, exposing yourself to their action, to the heartbeat of heaven and earth.

And do quit complaining about the weather! Quit disrespecting your Mother! Face every nuance with gratitude, with surprise, amazement, delight! Especially with gratitude, heartfelt, fervent gratefulness, for every drenching raindrop, every icicle, every sweltering ray of sun. Only when you can learn to be thankful for the features that cause inconvenience or pain can you truly be blessed by those features you do enjoy.

I am teaching you the secrets of evolution.

What is the level of urgency here? There is none. There is great need for transformation, but many forevers might pass with the need increasing, yet there would be no urgency.

Urgency distorts the real. Urgency collapses possibility and reduces potential to the shortest distance between two points. What is the problem with that? Quite simply: from point beginning-human to point completed-human, one cannot go in haste. One must traverse every inch of ground, and know every molecule between beginning and completion. No quick dash through the cafeteria. One cannot be satiated unless one has tasted and tested all the offerings, been filled many times, and is finally satisfied and quite ready to move away and into new modes of being, like the caterpillar, satisfied with its grand discoveries made in the cocoon and ready to break free, with wings; like the crocus, ready to leave its bulb and venture forth into the earth, the sunshine and the rain.

In order for the human being to venture from the cocoon, from the bulb, of its radical existence, it must be ready to move forward. If it comes from a place of "fight, flight, or freeze," seeking some sort of respite, or from weariness in well-doing, it has not traversed all the avenues encoded in the bulb, in the cocoon. One can only be satiated by experience over and over, an over-abundance of much experience, and then, furthermore, and in addition, upon the over-abundance is this qualification: One has demonstrated mastery. In every nuance, every shade, every trace, one has shown mastery -- of the situation? Of the circumstances? No! Such mastery drives one back into the cocoon, into the bulb. Then, what?

One has demonstrated mastery of one's own impulses. One has developed an objective, insatiable curiosity toward one's *self*. This *insatiable* curiosity will lead one *through* the experiences in the cocoon, in the bulb, in a manner which allows *objective* appraisal at every turn. Then one does not become mired in self-pity, fear, anger, sorrow, shame and the like. One moves quickly *out of* these conditions, fueled by *CURIOSITY*. Curiosity about what? Other people? Others' reactions, actions, feelings? The world? Turns of events? No! None of these things, and nothing else, save curiosity about one's *own inner* climate, one's own emotional responses to stimuli from the world. Curiosity about the inner landscape, which is the mindscape, the heartscape, *within one's own being.*

Dealing with feelings means feeling feelings. Be the witness, cooly appraising your own emotional weather, without judgment or comment, but with great interest and with *curiosity.* Know that the greater the pain in the feeling, the greater the opportunity for transformation, for transcendence. The inner secrecy of your heart is where universal transformation occurs. It is there that the determinations occur which convert expression into service and discover the path home.

In time-space an impulse from universal mind subjects itself to all emotional possibilities. Then it returns, a free, **knowing** spirit, bringing the gift of service, which is <u>wor-ship</u>... and please bear in mind that the root meaning of the word *worship* is merely the state of recognizing *worth.*

The return does not begin with deeds though deeds are of a certainty determined by the turnings in your secret hearts. The return begins in that secret place where free will holds sway, where human choice sends back the pure impulse impelled by the service of recognizing in awe and wonder the absolute, infinite worth of it all.

Thus the universe swings and flows, and thus universal mind gathers to itself a knowing along with its being. This is the process in which you participate as you convert expression into service, as you ferret out your impulses, recycling them with love by letting them tell their stories which, expressed, change death into life.

How close many religions come to the truth of this! Yet the truth is turned into its opposite if it doesn't come through the heart of the individual -- and it can only come through the heart if it is ferreted out from all possibilities through the device of folly. For folly is the wand that assures the freedom of the will in the choice. It cannot be clearer, save in the heart where our words cannot go.

The human condition has been thrown off via its reproductive system. Does this mean that sex is at the root of the human problem? No! What it means is that *parenting* throws people off. What it means is that when adults are responsible for the little ones, the adults tend to lose themselves in the responsibility, tossing away their curiosity about their own beings and immersing themselves in the supposed well-being of the offspring.

Curiosity is abundant in young children, until and unless it is squelched. Unchecked, it draws them through all their inner drives until, satiated, about the age of seven, they are ready to turn to transforming it to inventiveness, to become, each one, the great unique inventor -- if parents tended only the physical safety and nurturance of the child, diligently and fully, and offered nothing but unqualified acceptance of the child. But parents have been long caught up in monitoring the socialization of their children, the so-called moral well-being, the salvation of the child's "soul" at the expense of their own, and this is the greatest sell-out in history. And it does not begin in government seats or anywhere else but in the home, and in the nursery.

If parents were sufficiently curious about their own selves, at the inner level, they would be occupied there, would be free to support their children's own selves at that level, and would be content to do nothing for their children but provide complete and unlimited safety and nurturance.

But what happened is this: People of antiquity failed to tend their *own* inner fires (today we might say "files") through objective curiosity. Instead they attempted to subdue passion in others, and failing that, adults took on the easy task of subjugating passion as it might manifest in their infants and children.

Since curiosity, directed inward, is the key to transcending the human condition, loss of curiosity directed inward leads to moral mandates directed outward, and this is what has corrupted the human experience and literally "spoiled" our children -- not in the traditional sense, but in this sense: We have taken our beautiful, pure and unsoiled offspring and in a matter of a few short years, or even months or weeks, damaged them so that in a lifetime of effort they cannot extricate themselves from the bonds we have placed upon them. Some can; some have; many cannot or do not.

Now, what is the bright side? Can there be a bright side to such an entrenched, deleterious condition? Yes. If children had been raised so ideally throughout history, would we be aware of the value of such an upbringing? It would be the status quo, unquestioned, its value unknown. This is the benefit of curiosity. All possibilities are explored; all potentialities become known. And then choices can be made.

Children who come out of such deleterious modes of upbringing, and who then choose the way of curiosity-directed-within, need never fall prey to disinformation again. And that is how one moves into graduation from the human condition. One knows; one chooses; one moves forward within, and the movement propels one forward, and moving forward again, one checks the map, and ultimately reaches completion.

What about the children of these children? What about the children of the ones who raise them unspoiled, in conditions of total safety and nurturing, acceptance and support? Will they have to go through the process again, of falling prey to disinformation? Perhaps. And what is wrong with that? Nothing. But there is a fundamental miscalculation in the question. Children produced in the human condition are *in* the condition which imposes the spoiling. *When one has passed from the human condition to those conditions which remain yet nameless, one no longer reproduces in the human condition, hence one's offspring are not subject to the same vicissitudes.*

Yes, curiosity is the "oxylinear force field" that cuts through all the muck on the inner landscape and allows a clear picture to emerge, a picture which illumines the map one had at one's fingertips when one was born.

If you allow curiosity to do its work when you feel overwhelmed, or empty, or confused, afraid, upset, guilty, griefstruck, it will cut through the fog and the mist -- and through the garbage. (Remember that garbage was once the essential, pristine stuff of creation!) Curiosity allows you to poke your head, like the crocus, out of the dirt and into the light. It allows you to leave the nest, perhaps founder a bit, then take flight.

It is no accident or coincidence that curiosity and the word "cure" are derived from the same root. And what a cure! leading all the way through the ills of human life, right through it into the beyond! Wonder. Full of wonder. Wonder-ful. Curiosity. Yes. The cure. Don't negate it in the children. Let them have it. It is all they need to transcend, along with safety which you may provide, with support and nurturing. Start with your own child within.

The crucible for transcendence is the chalice and the blade, the stem and the petal, the candle and the candle holder, the goblet and the wine. Many fight transcendence not because they do not want to transcend, but because they do not recognize the tools, which drag them through all the pain and all the mud and toil they have not yet fully felt. They have resisted the painfulness and the isolation, mainly the isolation, because, like birth and like death, transcendence has to be done alone.

It is a beautiful Earth. And since the human condition is such that many vicissitudes, trials and challenges beset the being so journeying, it must be beautiful. Do you see that -- do you feel that -- an austere, forbidding environment would negate the story of the human being? Because of the arduous nature of the task of transcendence, there must be the relief of natural beauty such as is found on Earth.

How do distortions arrive in matter? Where do they enter? What about, for example, hatred, corruption, distortions of truth which amount to falsehood, hoodwinking masses of people through expanses of space-time? In the realm of soul/spirit the purity remains, for there is a willing and gracious receptacle for the impulse from universal mind. In mind/psyche, however, distortions can begin. The initial purity may be strengthened, or it may be sullied, weakened. If strengthened, emotion/motivation then receiving it, combines it with existing emotions and motivations, which in turn are uplifted by the incoming expression.

If, however, the impulse is weakened or sullied while in mind/psyche, emotion and motivation are hard put to redeem the impulse, and will receive it as a weight and a burden. The embodied human being, then, finds in life many emotional burdens to overcome, or in the alternative, to succumb to. There is a "short" and the return to universal mind through service is halted. Can this short be cured? New impulses are sent continuously.

While the natural world provides the beauty necessary to the process of transcendence, art supplies the means to internalize the beauty. Without the internalization, the beauty remains external to human experience and therefore does not actively lend itself to the transcendence. So do you see where we are now? Yes. Back at invention. Back at creativity. Back at the human inventory. And, yes, back to free will, yes, why, we are right back at folly!

Folly -- because the human being must be free to express artistically all the quirks and reaches of imagination -- back at free will, because the human being must be free to will its observation and experience into an individualized, unique form. We are back at the human inventory and back at invention.

So the earth is a hotbed of invention. What of other planets? Do you really want to know what can only be known to the transcender? What would blow your earthly mind? *Can* you know? *Could* you know?

Are you beginning to see the import of the need for transcendence? It is the portal. It is the passage, the Rubicon -- the river which, when crossed, allows for no return. (Or if you could return, you would have to recreate, reinvent, the conditions which would bring you back. Yours in this too is your own choice, your own folly.)

Transcendence is like the crocus. The bloom can only occur because of the inward process. Santa Claus could not make his trip around the world without the indoor process of the elves in the shop at the North Pole, and without all the sittings on his lap by the children whispering their wishes in his ear. The wedding cannot occur without the prior intimate exchanges between the two to be joined; the cap and gown cannot be donned without all the private study. Thus transcendence takes place privately, over perhaps immeasurable periods of time; its evidence is the final performance, the burst of fireworks that passes in a moment though it took centuries for the science of ballistics to develop the Roman candle.

Changing one's inner impetus, say, from worry and duty, fear and shame, from degradation and narcissism, bullying and controlling, from conformity and subservience or from any of the predominant inner stances of the human being to an inner stance of gratitude and celebration -- for no reason but for itself -- is this journey to the Rubicon.

The crossing then is evidence of the completed journey, up hill, down dale, through wind, snow, hail, sleet, sweltering heat, through lands occupied by enemies, death-defying, always life-affirming -- and oftentimes the affirmation of life entails the paradoxical act of jumping into the jaws of death.

Chapter Five

Universal mind is the egg; thought is the sperm.
Thoughts are myriad and skitter and caper,
seeking and running away,
while universal mind provides the grounding, the home base.
Thought contains the homing instinct
and universal mind provides the home.

The odd thing -- and here we are back at paradox -- is that transcendence cannot be done alone. Perhaps it should be said that transcendence must be done unassisted. Oh, there are assistants, galore, there are teachers, encouragers, many who cheer and applaud, but everyone must run the race alone. Yet according to Noah's story they pack into the vessel by two's. The male and female tigers who boarded the ark boarded alone yet together. One without the other would not have been admitted. So with human beings, one comes with one's companion in transcendence. For while the coming is solitary, yet there is the joining.

Only when you can learn to know the bliss of

solitude can you move forward and find the rest of yourself and enter into the alchemical union of two parts which were once separated for growth. In order to make a lemon meringue pie the whites of the eggs must be separated from the yolks. In order to have a beautiful Earth the land must be separated from the water. In order to have human evolution the male and female must be separated.

Did you think they were separated in order to procreate, to fill the earth with human bodies? No. There are other ways to do this. The male and female were separated from each other in order to have lemon meringue pie, in order to walk upon the land, enjoy the flowers, trees, mountains, waterfalls, in order to swim in the lake and dry in the warm sun on the shore. Male and female were separated in order to enjoy each other and in the search for one another to develop the separate parts. As the whites are beaten while the yolks are cooked with the sugar and lemon juice they evolve separately, yet always with each other in view, to ultimately join in a supremely new creation.

Is life, then, is human evolution nothing but an endless search and bumping into one another, having a dance, having a marriage, having a flirtation, an obsession with another, over and over and over again? No. There is an end in mind. There is an end in universal mind.

Androgyny is exactly what the word in its root meaning implies: man-woman. Andro-gyny. Many E.T.'s are androgynous, and it is said that "in heaven the angels do not marry nor are they given in marriage." Such "angels" and many E.T.'s have reached the point in evolution where the search and restless agitation, looking for the mate, has drawn to its close. There is rest. There is union. There is flawless satisfaction. This *follows* the rest found alone, without the mate. This *follows* the union found within a single human heart, often before the mate is even located.

Is this some kind of paradox? It certainly is. Because the rest and the union become a new story in the universe with every such joining, yet it does not negate the story of the excitation of the two finding each other.

For lack of the union *without* the mate the human race goes on and on, and on and on, with its futile self-destruction, ever making babies, as if the babies can grow up to do what the parents could not.

So, practice your folly! Do what you want to do anyway, which is to have the perfect mate, the perfect relationship, the one that fulfills your deepest yearnings and your highest dreamings. Just remember that you cannot truly find with another what you have not already become with yourself.

What has this to do with the human inventory? The EX-pression flows outward from universal mind and is characterized by separation into various parts and particles. The IM-pression flows inward. Expression requires male and female to be separate. Impression brings them inward to each other, where they are pressed together in the holy union caricaturized on Earth as marriage. Earthly marriage is like little children playing with wooden swords and miniature tea cups. When the real comes along you will know it, and you cannot be satisfied to return to your wooden swords and toy cups.

And if when that happens you are astute enough to

recognize it, you will know that the wholeness had to be in you first without your mate. If you are not whole alone, then that is what you must work toward, and this often occurs through practice relationships which take many forms. Remember, the number of stories is infinite. And love is living out your story without negating another's.

What if you are whole and your mate proves not to be? Or vice versa? Then the time is not right. Your own wholeness has more expression to do before it is ripe. For I tell you of a certainty that when you are completely ready for the union, your mate will be too. When the earth turns from night it does not come into another night but into day, and so the mates come together in perfect timing. It can be no other way.

What about accidents which separate those who seem to be perfectly joined? On Earth there are seeming accidents; here we see none. Experience on Earth affords the tests and circumstances needed; the true assessment of a relationship may dictate a round of grieving, or simply waiting in order to ripen what has already grown in the individual.

It is really quite simple. And beautiful. And quite simply it *is* the meaning of human life.

So now let us track the historical progression to this point in human evolution. During cave-dwelling times there was human mating. Some few transcended then, most others mated for reasons of survival, custom or hormones. During all times there have been those transcenders, unknown, because historians are unaware. The eagle does not announce her flight, and paired eagles do not advertise their mating in the air. They simply do it. There may be witnesses, but awestruck witnesses hold the sacred secret. Stories may be told, but advertisement sullies the sacred.

The method of couples coming together today is altogether new and quite momentous. For they come by mutual choice, not by choice of family, parents, not choice of the male, as have been the customs for long. Rather, through mutual choice they come together. This is a great step forward, allowing curiosity to join with folly, with free will, and with love. It could happen in other scenarios, but not with the same stress, the same challenge, the same mutual autonomy, the same knowingness, the same consciousness. And not with the mutuality.

No wonder there is so much confusion, so much heartache, heartbreak, misunderstanding around the issues of relationship. How momentous, important, groundbreaking the method is these days, accompanying the factor of so many souls, now, to learn transcendence. Of course it has to be learned with another; of course it has to be learned alone.

People mate -- all the time -- with one who is not their companion in transcendence. There is learning, hopefully, self-discovery, but not transcendence. The companion in transcendence is often on the fringes of one's life if at all, while one moves through self-discovery through following one's folly, through insatiable curiosity that drives one finally to the companion in transcendence, and then to the transcendence of the human condition. But first the curiosity must have done its complete work, the folly followed through the entirety of the maze, and then: A-Mazing Grace, how sweet the sound! The maze is reversed, straightened, unraveled, and there is clear passage ahead.

Why are there so many romances? In movies, in books, all around, and yet so few exemplary relationships? Because, simply, the transcending relationships are few, and they are most generally quiet. The learning relationships are many, and the trials and the errors abound and resound.

If you are involved in a learning relationship on the one hand, and on the other, in a transcending relationship, do not think yourself singled out. This is common. Follow the order as it has been explained in terms of love and of folly, and in terms of curiosity directed within. Do not negate another's story, rather live out a new one. In enhancing your own options, you inevitably enhance the numbers of options for all others in the situation.

The crux of the matter is this: The maze unwinds, the high fences collapse and form viewing platforms, the dark places are lighted and the wild places made accessible. This happens *when* the human being has unwound all the backward pathways and explored all the byways, taking in the scents, the sounds, the sights. *How* is this done? By -- yes -- by going within and enjoying the inner landscape, the emotional climate, by loving it as the lover cherishes the beloved. And I remind you here in this very context of the meaning of love: the allowing of all stories to be told, the heeding of all stories, the listening to all stories. Go within and cherish your own story, lived in the inner worlds, the world of emotion, the energy-in-motion in that sacred and holy place that is your own soul.

Now, how does *this* fit with the human inventory?

Do you see now how transcendence is a constant state of being, and what is called transcendence is actually the culmination, when the transcendence is finished? Transcendence is not a future; it is a present.

The sperm plunging into the egg and the two becoming one is the metaphor for human existence, also the metaphor for human transcendence. Therefore, sperm and egg are parts of the human inventory as well as the completion they symbolize. Sperm, the seeking half of human being, which also runs away, or, in time-space, *Being in perpetual motion*, and egg, the stable half of human being in time-space, which provides grounding, home base, *Being in stillness*. Universal mind is the egg; thought is the sperm. Thoughts are myriad and skitter and caper, seeking and running away, while universal mind provides the grounding, the home base, for calm and peace. Thought contains the homing instinct and universal mind provides the home.

What about the many sperm units which never find home in the egg? They are recycled, aren't they? Thus they remain a part of nature just as the many thoughts do which never find peace in universal mind. For the myriad recycled there is one which finds home, just as at certain moments there are thoughts which fly as arrows to their marks. And the task of human being is to join consciousness with this thought, and the next thought which flies to its mark, and the next, and so on.

Chapter Six

When the crocus finds itself buried in dirt with no light,
does it get depressed?
Of course it does. Then what does it do?
It explores. It goes searching into its environment,
not fighting the depression, but finding its own true nature
and ways to express it. It does not seek to change its nature,
which is to be buried in dirt. And from that burial,
from that depression, comes its real life.

How many children (of all ages) get what they really want from Santa Claus? How many people during the holidays drink themselves into oblivion, or avoid family or other gatherings, or participate with teeth-gritting endurance? Celebration at sporting events represents loss for the "losers." Birthdays are "celebrated" often as mere markers of the aging process which is so maligned in popular perception. How many wedding celebrations turn out to be simply expensive "bon voyage to joy" parties?

When did you last celebrate? Feel true joy? Natural euphoria? Glad rejoicing from your heart? Yet:

THERE IS CAUSE FOR NOTHING BUT CELE-

BRATION. Indeed, it is the vehicle for transcendence.

Celebration is the gathering together of energies into a combustible whole. The image of the whirling atom, all its components dancing ecstatically in synchronized wonder, is the image of celebration. The galaxies -- gala events in the universe -- are celebrations. These are not time-marked events but states of being into which one may enter and there dwell. The image of the butterfly, once flown from the cocoon and thereafter sky-dancing all its life, is an image of celebration. The ocean, waltzing shore to shore, is another. The line between day and night is another, as the sunrise, the sunset, travels endlessly along the edge of the earth.

The crocus bulb is in continuous celebration. How does it celebrate? It discovers. It unfolds. It reaches from its cocoon, its bulb, and discovers the moist and nurturing earth, explores its impulse toward the light, and its impulse toward the darkness. It sends its flower and leaves skyward, its roots downward, all in one sweep of celebration. When it blooms it explodes inward, continuing its celebration by swelling the bulb in preparation for more... "more," as the celebration proceeds from stage to stage, from state to state of being.

So, what prevents human beings from living in this continuous state of celebration? It is *de-pression*, which is the withholding of the *ex-pression* of an impulse.

Is it sometimes healthy to go ahead and really get into a depression that seems to overtake one? It can be, because depression is exacerbated by the withholding of its expression. Often when one begins to feel depressed one fights the feeling: Go buy a new hat, a new car, a new something-or-other, blame someone or something, get a new wife or husband, take the latest antidepressant, get drunk.

When the crocus finds itself buried in dirt with no light, does it get depressed? Of course it does. Then what does it do? It explores. It goes searching into its environment, not fighting the depression, but finding its own true nature, and ways to express it. It does not seek to change its nature, which is to be buried in dirt. And from that burial, from that depression, comes its real life.

Humans discover they are buried in dirt and get depressed. See what a crocus can teach you? Go exploring! What you see tells you that it explores its environment -- roots down, flower up -- but let me tell you the truth: It really explores *inward*. It goes inside its bulb and asks itself, "What's really inside here?" And the reason it is able to send its roots into the earth and its flower toward heaven is that when it goes inward it finds who it is.

Folly is what led the crocus inward. Folly and following the curiosity about its *own* nature. Preoccupation with *other* nature is what leads humans into depression. Preoccupation with the nature of disease, of upbringing, the nature of prejudice, of many another entity, other than one's own. What leads humans out of depression is, yes, it is expression. But before expression can occur, there must be, what? Exploration. And the exploration is the prelude to, yes, *CELEBRATION!*

What? With all the horrible things going on in the world? *Why yes!* Yes, yes, *YES!* All the more so! All of the horrible things going on in the world do not negate the crocus. Or the butterfly. Or the atom! Or the galaxies! Or the dirt, or the sun, or the expression!

And here we are back at invention. With all the horrible things going on in the world, invention can still occur! Yes, indeed. Invention had better occur! And depression does tend to stifle invention. What do the inventors do? They burrow through their emotions with great curiosity, with great gusto. They spend their emotions, every last penny; they do not hoard them. Hoarding of emotion leads to depression.

One does not have to burrow through all the horrible things around one. That would be like the earthworm obsessed with burrowing on Mars, stuck on Earth. A very depressed earthworm. The earthworm who is satisfied to burrow on Earth is burrowing through itself. And that is what the human must do. Not burrow elsewhere, but only through itself. Its environment merely stimulates the inner process. It is the inner process through which it burrows. Be like the earthworm and fulfill your nature! Outer stimuli are only that: stimulation for the inner process.

The earthworm would die without the earth. So the human being dies without the act of burrowing inward. One may last long but in a state of death, because where the worth really lies -- the only cause for celebration -- is unknown from the outside, and that is the greatest death. That, on the diagram of the human inventory, is the human being come to manifestation and sticking there.

The turning point inward is the turning from expression to service, service directed *through* emotion/motivation, *through* mind/psyche, *through* soul/spirit, and back to universal mind. To stay with expression when it is finally time to turn inward is to court depression, and death.

Let's talk about gratitude, the attitude leading to celebration, the vehicle for transcendence. When you lie sleepless in the night, beset by the many duties and nagging challenges of the day, gratitude is the way to go, the way to go off to sleep. Gratitude for what? Just gratitude, for nothing.

Oh, if you must connect the feeling of gratitude with something, then you certainly may. Be grateful for your little toe, if you have one. If not, find something else. Be ever so indulgently thankful for the faithfulness of your little toe, always at the end of your body, always supporting, always true to itself. Next be thankful for the little toe nail. What would that faithful toe do without the little nail? The toe is stabilized by the nail, as the body is stabilized by the toe.

You could be grateful for the sky, which provides you with the air you are breathing, and brings you so much beauty. How could one ever forget the beauty, and the sustenance? The lack of gratitude is the act of forgetting, which means "getting before gratitude." If you practice gratitude before you *get any* thing, you set the stage for a story of loving grace.

Would you come off a fool? You might. People might stare as you stand transfixed in the market before the bucket of flower bouquets. But never mind. Which is better? To stare in awe and gratitude at the beauty of the flowers? Or to stare in perplexity at the person staring in awe and gratitude at the flowers? Or at the shades of subtle color and the passing shapes in the clouds beyond the buildings and the utility wires and the steeples?

Did anyone ever get jailed for gratitude? Did anyone ever get fired for gratitude? Expelled from school? Divorced? You can burrow inward if you can't sleep, and inside you may be overwhelmed by the causes for gratitude -- the way your belly gently rises and falls with your breathing; the steady rhythm of your pulse in your throat; the way your legs lie so naturally along the length of the mattress; the gentle fold of your hands as they fall naturally on the pillow, or on your chest ... the miraculous way your eyelids slip over your eyes so that you can more easily slip inward.

The path of dreams is the inward path. The problems belong to the day, not to the night, to the waking world, not to the sleeping world. This is the use of boundaries, boundaries that shut out the problems and the nagging challenges, letting you explore inward and celebrate, so that when day comes again the gratitude of the night brings forth celebration and the overwhelming nature of the problems is overwhelmed by the nature of the celebration. You will see the results.

Where shall we go now? To hope?

Hope is the greatest of human folly, folly at its best. Hope is capable of engineering a path without the goal. Hope can be the vehicle for celebration and gratitude, without object, without attachment. Hope is the elixir, the medium for the medicine, the cure/curiosity which provides the ongoing condition of transcendence. Try it. Take it in as feeling, for feeling is the key. Remember that emotion is wedded to motivation, and since emotion/motivation is glued into time-and-space, propelling into matter the impulse seeking expression, emotion/motivation is also the gateway that propels one back toward universal mind.

Hope draws one's gaze to the light at the end of the tunnel, causing experience to take form as a tunnel rather than a prison cell. And, hope must be anchored within or it is not hope, but a fallacious faith. Why? Any belief anchored without oneself is a loose cannon, an asteroid careening dangerously through space.

The planets and suns turn on their own axes before they orbit around other bodies. So the human being must turn on its own center before it can dance. Then higher beings come into play, higher powers, suns, galactic centers and so forth. But first the human being must rotate upon its own axis, centered and whole within itself.

So how does hope work, if it is the greatest of all folly? Hope is the antenna which strengthens your attunement to celebration and gratitude. Add hope as your antenna, and celebration and gratitude will flow more easily and will ease your interface with life on planet Earth.

You have no grasp of the import, the importance, of *living* our admonitions. I say you have absolutely no grasp of the dire import of the necessity of incorporating all of this into your personal lives. You know this is true, and that time-space gives you the context to incorporate what you are learning. You know, but do you realize? Realizing means making real. *It is the difference between life and death, between heaven and hell.* What more can be said.

You stand at a critical juncture; the world hovers in the balance. Your personal lives converge at great crossroads. Think carefully, weigh wisely. But know, that eternity hangs on your every breath, your every hair's-breadth, your every heartbeat. Be big not small, be wide not narrow. Attend the invisible, the infinitesimal gap for it leads you to new worlds. It is the gate that swings between heaven and hell.

Why are there so many people in the world today? There is a gathering, a great and momentous conflagration of those who want to be in on the next wave of evolution. They know that to move from the human condition, they must be in the human condition. They have moved out of human bodies without spiritually advancing, so they must return to human bodies in order to transcend the human condition. Many lose the realization only to come upon it later in life, though once one glimpses this impetus to birth in one's history, one generally stays on the path of seeking the answers and formulas for the transcendence.

An interchange changes inwardly the parties involved, as opposed to an exchange, which involves outward change. So as we carry on these "interchanges," we are both changed inwardly. You know you are. I am, and you must take my word for that.

So. Where do we go from here? A revelation that is characterized by prophecy is one that frowns on folly. A revelation that is characterized by discovery and enlightenment is one that has come to terms with folly and learned to embrace it. "Prophecy" means to "profess" meaning or interpretation; "discovery and enlightenment" means to illumine that which is.

If all the material is studied and imbibed, every part taken equally with every other part, no more will be needed, only elaboration for every turn of folly in all the infinite givens yet to come in the lives of those who practice these models.

Is it knowledge, wisdom, or truth? What is the difference, really? *Knowledge* is the bark of the tree; *wisdom* is the sap and the juices, and *truth* is the archetypal tree to which every visible tree aspires.

This collection of words and concepts contains much knowledge to enhance learning. If you take it in and are nourished by it, it is wisdom. If you grasp the grand design and practice it, then it is truth.

Go for one, or go for all three. Or if you go for one, make it the third; make it truth and aspire to the whole of it. Go for the second, wisdom, and be fed by it; for the first, knowledge, and learn. I'd go for the three. That is, if you are ready to cross the Rubicon.

Other books from ARay Press:

EA 101 - We are Earth's Everlasting Arms in Embryo
Fables by the Sea
Ode to Earth in 9-11 Meter
Prisms and Songs for the Beloved
Sweet Influences - Voices from the Void
The Forest Dweller
The Gardener's Exile
The Nu I Ching
The Soul's Seasons - Gregorian to Mayan calendar
The Stickspeaker Collection
The World - before, now, to come (poetry)
Wings of Comfort - New Light on Old Scripture
88 Keys to Well-being - mental, emotional, spiritual
99 Passwords to Personal Power